Enduring Words

FOR
EVERYDAY
LIVING

Enduring Words

FOR

EVERYDAY
LIVING

School Specialty.
Publishing

Anthology: Margaret Miller
Design: Zoë Murphy

This anthology © The Five Mile Press Pty Ltd

This edition published in the United States in 2006 by School Specialty
Publishing, a member of the School Specialty Family.

Library of Congress Cataloging-in-Publication Data is on file with the publisher.

Send all inquiries to:

School Specialty Publishing
8720 Orion Place
Colombus, OH 43240-2111

ISBN 0-7696-4705-7

Printed in China
1 2 3 4 5 6 7 8 9 FMP 09 08 07 06 05

www.SchoolSpecialtyPublishing.com

CONTENTS

PREFACE

In the rush of modern life, too many of us are existing rather than living. Our lives often consist of work schedules, appointments, hastily snatched meals, and an evening in front of the television. It is important to stop to 'smell the roses,' to enjoy life to the fullest.

Some of life's greatest wonders are the simplest, most commonplace things, like a summer's morning, shady trees, or birds twittering at dusk. And many of its pleasures are equally ordinary: arranging a bowl of flowers from the garden, going for a solitary walk, or chatting with friends. And yet, how often do we stop to think about, and appreciate, those experiences? The passages in this endearing anthology help us to look at life with fresh eyes, to 'seize the day,' and to reflect on what is important.

By its very nature, life is full of change, and new challenges constantly come our way. As this book's many wise reflections confirm, it is how we respond to life's hardships that matters most.

Whatever stresses you face, you can always take the time to get in touch with your innermost self, to enjoy the company of friends, and to delight in nature. As the Chinese philosopher Loy Chin-Yuen wrote, 'An inch of time is an inch of gold: Treasure it.'

Seize the Day!

$\mathcal{L}$ook to this day.

In it lie all the realities and verities of existence,

the bliss of growth, the splendor of action,

the glory of power.

For yesterday is but a dream

and tomorrow is only a vision.

But today, well-lived,

makes every yesterday a dream of happiness

and every tomorrow a vision of hope.

—————
Sanskrit proverb

*E*ach soul must meet the morning sun,

the new sweet earth,

and the Great Silence.

Ohiyesha (Charles Alexander Eastman), 1858–1939
American author, physician

Light tomorrow with today.

Elizabeth Barrett Browning, 1806–1861
English poet

*W*hen I begin to sit

with the dawn in solitude,

I begin to really live.

It makes me treasure

every single moment of life.

Gloria Vanderbilt, b. 1924
American socialite, artist

$\mathcal{N}$othing

is worth more

than this day.

Johann von Goethe, 1749–1832
German novelist, philosopher

*A*sk not what tomorrow may bring,

but count as blessing

every day that Fate allows you.

Horace, 65–8 BC
Italian poet

*D*o not dwell in the past.

Do not dream of the future.

Concentrate the mind

on the present moment.

Buddha, c. 500 BC
Indian philosopher, founder of Buddhism

*Y*ou have to live on this earth

twenty-four hours of daily time.

Out of it, you have to spin health,

pleasure, money, content, respect, and

the evolution of your immortal soul.

Its right use, most effective use,

is a matter of the highest urgency and

of the most thrilling actuality.

All depends on that.

We shall never have any more time.

Arnold Bennett, 1867–1931
English novelist

$\mathcal{L}$ook at a day when you are

supremely satisfied at the end.

It's not a day when you've lounged around

doing nothing.

It's when you've had everything to do,

and you've done it.

Lord Acton, 1834–1902
English historian

Happy the man, and happy he alone,

He who can call today his own:

He who, secure within, can say

Tomorrow do thy worst,

For I have lived today.

John Dryden, 1631–1700
English poet, playwright

*R*edeem thy misspent time that's past;

Live this day as if 'twere thy last.

—————————

Thomas Ken, 1637–1711
English bishop

Until you value yourself,

you won't value your time.

Until you value your time,

you will not do anything with it.

M. Scott Peck, b. 1936
American psychiatrist, writer

O gift of God! A perfect day,

Whereon no man should work but play,

Whereon it is enough for me,

Not to be doing but to be.

Henry Wadsworth Longfellow, 1807–1882
American poet

We are here and it is now.

Further than that,

all human knowledge

is moonshine.

H. L. Mencken, 1880–1956
American journalist, social critic

As yesterday is history

and tomorrow may never come,

I have resolved from this day on,

I will do all the business I can honestly,

have all the fun I can reasonably,

do all the good I can do willingly,

and save my digestion by thinking pleasantly.

Robert Louis Stevenson, 1850–1894
English novelist, poet

$\mathcal{T}$ime is the coin of your life.

It is the only coin you have, and only you

can determine how it will be spent.

Be careful lest you let other people

spend it for you.

Carl Sandberg, 1878–1967
American poet

A man can only do

what a man can do.

But if he does that each day,

he can sleep at night

and do it again the next day.

Albert Schweitzer, 1875–1965
German theologian, physician

*O*ut of Eternity,

the new Day is born.

Into Eternity,

at night will return.

Thomas Carlyle, 1795–1881
Scottish essayist, historian, philosopher

When you arise in the morning,

give thanks for the morning light.

Give thanks for your life and strength.

Give thanks for the joy of living.

And if perchance you see no reason

for giving thanks,

rest assured the fault is in yourself.

Native American saying

Finish each day and be done with it.

You have done all you could.

Some blunders and absurdities have crept in;

forget them as soon as you can.

Tomorrow is a new day;

you shall begin it serenely and with

too high a spirit to be encumbered

with your old nonsense.

Ralph Waldo Emerson, 1803–1882
American poet, essayist, teacher

Each morning sees some task begun;

Each evening sees it close.

Something attempted, something done,

Has earned a night's repose.

Henry Wadsworth Longfellow, 1807–1882
American poet

Write in your heart

that every day

is the best day of the year.

Ralph Waldo Emerson, 1803–1882
American poet, essayist, teacher

It is only when we truly know and understand

that we have a limited time on earth –

and that we have no way of knowing

when our time is up – that we will begin

to live each day to its fullest,

as if it were the only one we had.

Elisabeth Kübler-Ross, 1926–2004
Swiss-born American psychiatrist, writer

To Thine Own Self Be True

$\mathcal{T}$his above all – to thine own self be true,

And it must follow, as night follows day,

Thou canst not then be false to any man.

William Shakespeare, 1564–1616
English playwright, poet

*W*hat's originality?

It is being one's self

and reporting accurately

what we see.

Ralph Waldo Emerson, 1803–1882
American poet, essayist, teacher

*E*very individual has

a place to fill in the world,

and is important, in some respect,

whether he chooses to be or not.

***

Nathaniel Hawthorne, 1804–1864
American novelist

No one can make you feel inferior

without your own consent.

Eleanor Roosevelt, 1884–1962
First Lady of the United States of America

$\mathcal{T}$o be nobody but yourself –

in a world which is doing its best, night and day,

to make you like everybody else –

means to fight the hardest battle

which any human being can fight,

and never stop fighting.

---

e.e. cummings, 1894–1963
American poet

If I try to be like him,

who will be like me?

Jewish proverb

Don't surrender your individuality,

which is your greatest agent of power,

to the customs and conventionalities that

have got their life from the great mass ....

Do you want to be a power in the world?

Then be yourself.

Ralph Waldo Trine, 1866–1958
American poet, writer

There are big dogs and little dogs,

but the little dogs

should not be disheartened by

the existence of big dogs.

All must bark, and bark with

the voice God gave them.

Anton Chekhov, 1860–1904
Russian dramatist, writer

*A*lways be a

first-rate version of yourself

instead of a second-rate version

of somebody else.

Judy Garland, 1922–1969
American singer, actress

What's man's first duty?

The answer's brief: to be himself.

Henrik Ibsen, 1828–1906
Norwegian writer, dramatist, poet

One has just to be oneself.

That's my basic message.

The moment you accept yourself as you are,

all burdens, all mountainous burdens,

simply disappear.

Then, life is a sheer joy,

a festival of lights.

Bhagwan Shree Rajneesh, 1931–1990
Indian spiritual master

*I*t is difficult to make

a man feel miserable

when he feels he is

worthy of himself.

Abraham Lincoln, 1809–1865
President of the United States of America

$\mathcal{B}$eing myself includes

taking risks with myself,

taking risks on new behavior,

trying new ways of 'being myself,'

so that I can see who it is I want to be.

Hugh Prather, b.1938
American writer

$\mathscr{R}$esolve to be thyself;

and know that he who finds himself

loses his misery.

Matthew Arnold, 1822–1888
British poet, essayist

$\mathcal{R}$eason is your light

and your beacon of Truth.

Reason is the source of Life.

God has given you Knowledge

so that by its light

you may not only worship Him,

but also see yourself in your

weaknesses and strength.

Kahlil Gibran, 1883–1898
Lebanese poet, artist, mystic

Change and Growth

To be what we are
and to become what
we are capable of becoming
is the only end in life.

Robert Louis Stevenson, 1850–1894
Scottish author, poet

We must always change,

renew, rejuvenate ourselves;

otherwise, we harden.

Johann von Goethe, 1749–1832
German poet, writer

$\mathcal{O}$nly in growth, reform, and change,

paradoxically enough,

is true security to be found.

Anne Morrow Lindbergh, 1906–2001
American aviator, writer

*L*ife is change.

Growth is optional.

Choose wisely.

Karen Kaiser Clark, b. 1938
American legislator, feminist

We shrink from change; yet is there anything

that can come into being without it?

What does Nature hold dearer

or more proper to herself?

Could you have a hot bath

unless firewood underwent some change? ...

Do you not see, then,

that change in yourself is of the same order

and no less necessary to Nature.

———————

Marcus Aurelius, 121–180 AD
Roman emperor, philosopher

The creation of a thousand forests

is in one acorn.

Ralph Waldo Emerson, 1803–1882
American poet, essayist, teacher

The old woman

I shall become

will be quite different

from the woman I am now.

Another I is beginning.

George Sand, 1804–1876
French writer, dramatist

*Real development
is not leaving things behind,
as on a road,
but drawing life from them,
as on a root.*

G.K. Chesterton, 1874–1936
English writer

To learn, to desire, to know,

to feel, to think, to act.

This is what I want.

And nothing else.

That is what I must try for.

Katherine Mansfield, 1888–1923
New Zealand short story writer

$\mathscr{E}$very small positive change

we make in ourselves

repays us in confidence

in the future.

Alice Walker, b. 1944
American author

Who is not satisfied

with himself

will grow.

Hebrew proverb

*T*he great law of culture is:

Let each become all

that he was created capable of being.

Thomas Carlyle, 1795–1881
Scottish essayist, historian, philosopher

*L*ove not what you are

but what you may become.

Miguel De Cervantes, 1547–1616
Spanish writer

$\mathcal{Y}$ou must learn day by day, year by year,

to broaden your horizons.

The more things you love,

the more you are interested in,

the more you enjoy,

the more you are indignant about –

the more you have left

if anything goes wrong.

Ethel Barrymore, 1879–1959
American entertainer

*I*f our nature

is permitted to guide our life,

we grow healthy,

fruitful, and happy.

Abraham Maslow, 1908–1970
American psychologist

$\mathcal{B}$e not afraid of

growing slowly.

Be afraid of

standing still.

Chinese proverb

*W*hen I stand before God

at the end of my life,

I would hope that I would not have

a single bit of talent left and could say,

'I used everything you gave me.'

Erma Bombeck, b. 1927
American writer, humorist

*My business
is not to remake myself,
but make the absolute best
of what God made me.*

Robert Browning, 1812–1889
English poet, playwright

*E*xamine myself as I may,

I can no longer find

the slightest trace of the anxious,

agitated individual of those years,

so discontented with herself,

so out of patience with others.

George Sand, 1804–1876
French writer

$\mathcal{W}$e deem those happy

who from the experience of life

have learned to bear its ills

without being overcome by them.

Carl Jung, 1875–1961
Swiss psychiatrist

The real voyage of discovery

consists not in seeking new landscapes

but in having new eyes.

Marcel Proust, 1871–1922
French writer

If we did all the things

we are capable of doing,

we would truly astound ourselves.

Thomas Edison, 1847–1931
American inventor

*T*he only way

to make sense out of change

is to plunge with it,

move with it,

and join the dance.

Alan Watts, 1915–1973
English philosopher

Chasing the Blues Away

$\mathcal{T}$hat is part of
the beauty of all literature:
You discover that your longings
are universal longings,
that you're not lonely
and isolated from anyone.
You belong.

F. Scott Fitzgerald, 1896–1940
American novelist

The best remedy for those

who are afraid, lonely, or unhappy

is to go outside, somewhere where

they can be quite alone with

the heavens, nature, and God.

Anne Frank, 1929–1945
Dutch schoolgirl, diarist

How to be happy

when you are miserable:

Plant Japanese poppies

with cornflowers and mignonette,

and set out the petunias among the

sweet-peas so they shall scent each other.

See the sweet-peas coming up.

Rumer Godden, 1907–1998
English writer

$\mathscr{I}$ will tell you what

I have learned for myself.

For me, a long five or six mile walk helps.

And one must go alone

and every day.

Brenda Ueland, 1891–1986
American writer

Gardening, even if it's only a few pots on
a balcony, is a wonderful antidote to anxiety.
So, I find, is a long, hard walk.
And here's a special tip: Try finding a place where
you can lie on your back and look, for a long time,
at the sky. The sky is always there, free for everyone.

Pamela Bone, b. 1950
Australian journalist

*T*he best way

to cheer yourself up

is to cheer someone else up.

_____

Mark Twain, 1835–1910
American writer, humorist

*I*t is almost

impossible to remember

how tragic a place the world is

when one is playing golf.

Robert Lynd, 1879–1949
Irish essayist, journalist

Noble deeds and hot baths
are the best cures for depression.

Dobie Smith, 1896–1990
English writer

*We can be cured of depression
in only fourteen days
if every day we will try to think
of how we can be helpful to others.*

Alfred Adler, 1870–1937
Austrian psychiatrist

*D*rink tea

and forget the world's noises.

———————

Chinese saying

*W*hether living alone is adventure or hardship
will depend entirely on your attitude and your decisions.
Become friends with yourself; learn to appreciate
who you are and your unique gifts.
Be patient with yourself and use your sense of humor
to keep things in perspective.

Dorothy Edgerton, b. 1911
American writer

The best antidote I have found

is to yearn for something.

As long as you yearn, you can't congeal;

there is a forward motion about yearning.

Gail Godwin, b. 1937
American writer

I have sometimes been wildly,

despairingly, acutely miserable,

racked with sorrow,

but through it all I still know

that just to be alive

is a grand thing.

Dame Agatha Christie, 1890–1976
English detective story writer, playwright

Delight in Simple Things

Teach us delight in simple things

And mirth that has no bitter springs,

Forgiveness free of evil done,

And love to all men 'neath the sun.

Rudyard Kipling, 1865–1936
Indian-born English writer, poet

$\mathscr{T}$here are two ways to live your life.

One is as though nothing is a miracle.

The other is as though everything is a miracle.

Albert Einstein, 1879–1955
German-born American scientist

The secret of seeing things as they are
is to take off our colored spectacles.
That being-as-it-is,
with nothing extraordinary about it,
nothing wonderful,
is the great wonder.

———————
Zen wisdom

*W*hat a delight it is

　　When, of a morning,

I get up and go out

　　To find in full bloom

A flower that yesterday

　　Was not there.

Tachibana Akemi, 1812–1868
Japanese poet

$\mathcal{W}$hy, who makes so much of a miracle?

As to me, I know nothing else but miracles –

To me, every hour of night and day is a miracle;

Every cubic inch of space is a miracle.

Walt Whitman, 1819–1891
American poet

*M*ay I a small house

And large garden have.

And a few Friends,

And many Books,

Both true, both wise,

And both delightful, too.

Abraham Cowley, 1618–1667
English poet

*H*e is the happiest,

be he king or peasant,

who finds peace in his home.

Johann von Goethe, 1749–1832
German poet, writer

*O*ne is nearer God's heart

in a garden

than anywhere else on earth.

<hr>

Dorothy Frances Gurney, 1858–1932
English poet

Look to your health;

and if you have it, praise God,

and value it next to a good conscience;

for health is the second blessing

that we mortals are capable of,

a blessing that money cannot buy.

Izaak Walton, 1593–1683
English writer

$\mathcal{L}$ife is made up of small pleasures.

Happiness is made up of those tiny successes.

The big ones come too infrequently.

And if you don't collect all these tiny successes,

the big ones don't really mean anything.

Norman Lear, b. 1922
American television writer, producer

I like to walk about among

the beautiful things that adorn the world;

but private wealth I should decline,

or any sort of personal possessions,

because they would take away my liberty.

George Santayana, 1863–1952
Spanish-born American philosopher, writer

*T*he day, water, sun, moon, night –

I do not have to pay to enjoy these things.

Titus Maccius Platus, c. 254–184 BC
Roman dramatist

I loved the house,

the way you would like any new house, because it was populated by your future – the family or children who will fill it with noise or chaos and satisfying busy pleasure.

Jane Smiley, b. 1949
American novelist

If I had two loaves of bread,

I would sell one and buy hyacinths.

For they would feed my soul.

The Qur'an

*M*y kitchen is a mystical place,

a kind of temple for me.

It is a place where the sounds and odors

carry meaning that transfers from the past

and bridges to the future.

Pearl Bailey, 1918–1986
American singer

Yes, in the poor man's garden grow

Far more than herbs and flowers –

Kind thoughts, contentment, peace of mind,

And joy for weary hours.

Mary Howitt, 1799–1888
English author

True love ennobles and dignifies

the material labors of life;

and homely services rendered for love's sake

have in them a poetry that is immortal.

Harriet Beecher Stowe, 1811–1896
American writer, abolitionist

China tea, the scent of hyacinths,

wood fires, and bowls of violets –

that is my mental picture

of an agreeable February afternoon.

Constance Spry, 1886–1960
British florist, author

*'M*id pleasures and palaces

we may roam.

Be it ever so humble,

there's no place like home.

J.H. Payne, 1791–1852
American dramatist, poet, actor

Who loves a garden still his Eden keeps,

perennial pleasures, plants, and

wholesome harvest reaps.

Amos Bronson Alcott, 1799–1888
American teacher, philosopher

I got up at sunrise and was happy;

I walked and was happy; I roamed the forests and hills;

I wandered in the valleys; I read; I did nothing;

I worked in the garden; I picked fruit;

I helped in the house; and happiness followed me

everywhere – happiness which could not be referred to

any definite object but dwelt entirely within myself

and which never left me a single instant.

Jean-Jacques Rousseau, 1712–1778
French philosopher

$\mathcal{Q}$uiet by day, sound sleep by night,

Study and ease together mixed,

Sweet recreation, and innocence,

Which most doth please

With meditation.

Alexander Pope, 1688–1744
English poet

*W*hat a delight it is

When I blow away the ash,

To watch the crimson

Of the glowing fire

And hear the water boil.

Tachibana Akemi, 1812–1868
Japanese poet

$\mathcal{N}$o place is more delightful

than one's own fireside.

Cicero, 106–43 BC
Roman orator, statesman, writer

$\mathcal{T}$he first fall of snow

is not only an event,

it is a magical event.

You go to bed in one kind of a world

and wake up in another quite different,

and if this is not enchantment,

then where is it to be found.

J.B. Priestley, 1894–1984
English writer, dramatist, critic

$\mathscr{I}$ would like to thank…

the birds outside my window

who constantly reassured me

that nothing is desperately important

and the joy of life is just looking at it.

Alec Guinness, 1914–2000
English actor

$\mathcal{G}$ive me books, fruit,

French wine, and fine weather,

and a little music out of doors

played by someone I don't know.

John Keats, 1795–1821
English poet

$\mathcal{S}$ummer is delicious; rain is refreshing;

wind braces us; snow is exhilarating;

there is no such thing as bad weather,

only different kinds of good weather.

John Ruskin, 1819–1900
English author, poet

O health! Health is the blessing

Of the rich!

The riches of the poor!

Who can buy thee

At too dear a rate,

Since there is no enjoying

This world without thee?

Ben Jonson, 1573–1637
English dramatist, poet

*M*ake Time for Solitude

*S*olitude is as needful

to the imagination

as society is wholesome

for the character.

James Russell Lowell, 1819–1891
American poet, essayist, diplomat

It is only in solitude

that men and women can come to know

the happiness that is like the delight of children

in nothing at all.

John Cowper Powys, 1872–1963
English novelist, essayist, poet

*A*rranging a bowl of flowers in the morning

can give a sense of quiet in a crowded day –

like writing a poem or saying a prayer.

What matters is that one be for a time

inwardly attentive.

Anne Morrow Lindbergh, 1906–2001
American aviator, writer

The goal of a healthy solitude is love —

love and acceptance of ourselves

as we are and where we are

and love and compassion for others.

Dorothy Payne, 1887–1968
American philanthropist, social activist

The most valuable thing

we can do for the psyche, occasionally,

is to let it rest, wander,

live in the changing light of a room,

not try to be or do anything whatever.

May Sarton, 1912–1995
American poet, writer

$\mathcal{T}$here's no need to go to India

or anywhere else to find peace.

You will find that deep place of silence

right in your own room,

your garden,

or even your bathtub.

Elisabeth Kübler-Ross, 1926–2004
Swiss-born American psychiatrist, writer

In solitude,

we give passionate attention to our lives,

to our memories,

to the details around us.

Virginia Woolf, 1882–1941
English novelist

*S*olitude – walking alone,

doing things alone –

is the most blessed thing in the world.

The mind relaxes and thoughts begin to flow,

and I think that I am beginning

to find myself a little.

Helen Hayes, 1900–1993
American actress

*T*he most important education you get

is your own – the one you learn

in solitude.

Erica Jong, b. 1942
American writer, poet

*W*ithin yourself

is a stillness and a sanctuary

to which you can retreat at any time

and be yourself.

Hermann Hesse, 1877–1962
German writer

*O*nly those

who learn how to live with solitude

can come to know themselves and life.

I go out there and walk and

look at the trees and sky. I listen.

I sit on a rock or a stump and say to myself,

'Who are you, Sandburg?

Where have you been, and what are you doing?'

Carl Sandburg, 1878–1967
American poet

One of the pleasantest

things in the world

is going on a journey;

but I like to go by myself.

William Hazlitt, 1778–1830
British essayist

But women need solitude in order

to find the true essence of themselves,

that firm strand which will be the indispensable

center of a whole web of human relationships.

Anne Morrow Lindbergh, 1906–2001
American aviator, writer

I am sure of this,

that by going much alone

a man will get more of a noble courage

in thought and word

than from all the wisdom that is in books.

Ralph Waldo Emerson, 1803–1882
American poet, essayist, teacher

I come to my solitary woodland walk

as the homesick go home.

Henry David Thoreau, 1817–1862
American essayist, writer

Sit quietly doing nothing.
Spring comes and the grass
grows by itself.

———————

Zen wisdom

*T*ruth is within ourselves; it takes no rise

From outward things, what'er you may believe.

There is an inmost center in us all,

Where truth abides in fullness.

Robert Browning, 1812–1889
English poet, playwright

This is what is strange – that friends,

even passionate love, are not my real life

unless there is time alone

in which to discover what is happening

or has happened.

May Sarton, 1912–1995
American poet, writer

You do not need to leave your room.

Remain sitting at your table and listen.

Do not even listen, simply wait.

Do not even wait, be still and solitary.

The world will freely offer itself to you

to be unmasked; it has no choice.

It will roll in ecstasy at your feet.

Franz Kafka, 1883–1924
Czechoslovakian-born writer

Teach us to care and not to care.

Teach us to sit still.

T. S. Eliot, 1888–1965
American-born British poet, critic

*M*y home is my retreat
and resting-place from the wars.
I try to keep this corner as a haven
against the tempest outside,
as I do another corner
of my soul.

Michel de Montaigne, 1533–1592
French writer, essayist

Friendship and Laughter

$\mathscr{A}$mong those whom I like or admire,

I can find no common denominator,

but among those I love, I can:

All of them make me laugh.

W. H. Auden, 1909–1973
English poet

$\mathcal{Y}$ou can always tell a real friend:

When you've made a fool of yourself,

he doesn't feel you've done

a permanent job.

Laurence J. Peter, 1919–1990
Canadian writer

*L*aughter has something in it in common with

the ancient winds of faith and inspiration:

It unfreezes pride and unwinds secrecy;

it makes men forget themselves in the presence

of something greater than themselves,

something that they cannot resist.

G.K. Chesterton, 1874–1936
English novelist, critic

*It's impossible
to speak highly enough of the virtues,
the dangers, and the power
of shared laughter.*

Françoise Sagan, 1935–2004
French novelist

And in the sweetness of friendship,

let there be laughter and sharing of pleasures.

For in the dew of little things,

the heart finds its morning

and is refreshed.

Kahlil Gibran, 1883–1931
Lebanese poet, artist, mystic

*T*rue friendship

is a plant of slow growth

and must undergo and withstand

the shocks of adversity before it is

entitled to the appellation.

George Washington, 1732–1799
President of the United States of America

The antidote for fifty enemies

is one friend.

Aristotle, 384–322 BC
Greek philosopher

$\mathcal{T}$he proper office of a friend

is to side with you

when you are in the wrong.

Nearly anybody will side with you

when you are in the right.

Mark Twain, 1835–1910
American writer

*I*t is one of the

blessings of friends

that you can afford to be

stupid with them.

Ralph Waldo Emerson, 1803–1882
American poet, essayist, teacher

True happiness consists

not in the multitude of friends,

but in the worth and choice.

Ben Jonson, 1573–1637
English dramatist, poet

I always felt

that the great high privilege,

relief, and comfort of friendship

was that one had to explain nothing.

Katherine Mansfield, 1888–1923
New Zealand short story writer

$\mathcal{T}$he better part of one's life

consists of one's friendships.

Abraham Lincoln, 1809–1865
President of the United States of America

*I*f you want people

to be glad to meet you,

you must be glad to meet them –

and show it.

Johann von Goethe, 1749–1832
German poet, writer, scientist

*I*f your face brightens

when you meet your friend,

you have struck gold.

Unknown

$\mathcal{F}$or whoever knows

how to return a

kindness he has received

must be a friend above price.

Sophocles, c. 496–406 BC
Greek tragedian

A real friend is

one who walks in

when the rest of the world

walks out.

Walter Winchell, 1879–1972
American journalist

I want someone to laugh with me,

someone to be grave with me,

someone to please me

and help my discrimination

with his or her remark,

and at times, no doubt, to admire

my acuteness and penetration.

Robert Burns, 1759–1796
Scottish poet

*O*ne's friends

are that part of the human race

with which one can be human.

George Santayana, 1863–1952
Spanish-born American philosopher, writer

Friendship consists in

forgetting what one gives

and remembering what one receives.

Alexandre Dumas, 1803–1870
French novelist

$\mathcal{U}$nder the magnetism of friendship,

the modest man becomes bold;

the shy, confident; the lazy, active;

or the impetuous,

prudent and peaceful.

William Makepeace Thackeray, 1811–1863
English writer

Each new friend represents a world in us,

a world possibly not born until they arrive,

and it is only by the meeting

that a new world is born.

Anaïs Nin, 1903–1977
French novelist

*I*f a man

does not make new acquaintance

as he advances through life,

he will soon find himself alone.

A man, sir, should keep his friendship

in constant repair.

Samuel Johnson, 1709–1784
English lexicographer, critic, essayist

We take care of our health;

we lay up money; we make our room tight

and our clothing sufficient;

but who provides wisely

that he shall not be wanting

in the best property of all – friends?

Ralph Waldo Emerson, 1803–1882
American poet, essayist, teacher

$\mathscr{F}$riendship improves happiness and abates misery

by doubling our joy and dividing our grief.

Joseph Addison, 1672–1719
English essayist

*F*rom quiet home and first beginning,

Out to the undiscovered ends,

There's nothing worth the wear of winning,

But laughter and the love of friends.

Hilaire Belloc, 1870–1953
English writer

Problems Aren't All Bad

$\mathcal{I}$'m grateful for all my problems.

As each of them was overcome,

I became stronger and more able

to meet those yet to come.

I grew on my difficulties.

J.C. Penney, 1875–1971
American retailing magnate

If there were

nothing wrong in the world,

there wouldn't be anything

for us to do.

George Bernard Shaw, 1856–1950
Irish dramatist, essayist, critic

A problem well stated

is a problem half solved.

Charles Franklin Kettering, 1876–1958
American engineer, inventor

*A*ll things are difficult

before they are easy.

Thomas Fuller, 1608–1661
English churchman, historian

I think these difficult times have
helped me to understand better than before
how infinitely rich and beautiful life is in
every way and that so many things one
goes around worrying about are
of no importance whatsoever.

Isak Dinesen, 1885–1962
Danish writer

Problems call forth

our courage and our wisdom; indeed,

they create our courage and our wisdom.

It is only because of problems

that we grow mentally and spiritually.

It is through the pain of

confronting and resolving problems

that we learn.

M. Scott Peck, b. 1936
American psychiatrist, writer

Adversity has the same effect on a man

that severe training

has on the pugilist –

it reduces him to his fighting weight.

Josh Billings, 1818–1885
American humorist

A man of character

finds a special attractiveness in difficulty

since it is only by coming to grips with difficulty

that he can realize his potentialities.

Charles de Gaulle, 1890–1970
French statesman, general

$\mathcal{L}$ife affords no higher pleasure

than that of surmounting difficulties,

passing from one step of success to another,

forming new wishes and seeing them gratified.

Samuel Johnson, 1709–1784
English lexicographer, critic, essayist

*C*haracter

consists of what you do

on the third and fourth tries.

James A. Michener, 1907–1997
American writer

The hill, though high, I covet to ascend;

The difficulty will not offend,

For I perceive the way to life lies here.

Come, pluck up heart, let's neither faint nor fear;

Better, though difficult, the right way to go,

Than wrong, though easy,

Where the end is woe.

John Bunyan, 1628–1688
English writer, moralist

$\mathcal{T}$hose things that hurt,

instruct.

Benjamin Franklin, 1705–1790
American statesman, scientist

I could do nothing without my problems;

they toughen my mind.

In fact, I tell my assistants

not to bring me their successes

for they weaken me

but rather to bring me their problems

for they strengthen me.

Charles Franklin Kettering, 1876–1958
American engineer, inventor

*D*o what is easy

as if it were difficult

and what is difficult

as if it were easy.

Baltasar Gracian, 1601–1658
Spanish priest

$\mathcal{H}$e knows not his own strength
that hath not met adversity.

Ben Jonson, 1573–1637
English dramatist

How to Be Happy

One is happy as a result of one's own efforts, once one
knows the necessary ingredients of happiness – simple tastes,
a certain degree of courage, self-denial to a point, love of work,
and above all, a clear conscience. Happiness is no vague dream.

George Sand, 1804–1876
French novelist

*M*ost people are about as happy
as they make up their minds to be.

Abraham Lincoln, 1809–1865
President of the United States of America

The great essentials

to happiness in this life

are something to do, something to love,

and something to hope for.

Joseph Addison, 1672–1719
English essayist

*H*appiness is a butterfly which,

when pursued, is always beyond our grasp,

but which, if you sit down quietly,

may alight upon you.

Nathaniel Hawthorne, 1804–1864
American writer

The happiest people seem to be
those who are producing something;
the bored people are those
who are consuming much
and producing nothing.

William Inge, 1860–1954
English prelate, writer

The secret of happiness

is not in doing what one likes

but in liking what one has to do.

J.M. Barrie, 1860–1937
Scottish writer, dramatist

*If you want to understand
the meaning of happiness,
you must see it as a reward
and not as a goal.*

Antoine de Saint-Exupery, 1900–1944
French writer, aviator

*I*f only we'd stop trying to be happy,

we could have a pretty good time.

Edith Wharton, 1862–1937
American novelist

Happiness arises in the first place

from the enjoyment of one's self

and, in the next,

from the friendship and conversations

with a few select companions.

Joseph Addison, 1672–1719
English essayist

The happiness of life

is made up of minute fractions.

The little soon-forgotten charities of a kiss or smile,

a kind look, a heartfelt compliment –

countless infinitesimals of

pleasurable and genial feelings.

Samuel Taylor Coleridge, 1772–1834
English poet

I suspect that the happiest people you know

are the ones who work at being kind,

helpful, and reliable – and happiness

sneaks into their lives while

they are busy doing those things.

It is a by-product, never a primary goal.

Harold S. Kushner
American rabbi

I don't know what your destiny will be;

but one thing I know:

The only ones among you who will be really happy

are those who will have sought and found

how to serve.

Albert Schweitzer, 1875–1965
French medical missionary

There are as many nights as days,

and the one is just as long as the other

in the year's course.

Even a happy life cannot be without

a measure of darkness, and the word 'happy'

would lose its meaning if it were not

balanced by sadness.

Carl Jung, 1875–1961
Swiss psychiatrist

*H*e who wishes

to secure the good of others

has already secured his own.

Confucius, c. 550–478 BC
Chinese philosopher

$\mathcal{T}$he secret of happiness is this:

Let your interests be as wide as possible,

and let your reactions to the things and

persons that interest you be as far as possible

friendly rather than hostile.

Bertrand Russell, 1872–1970
English philosopher, mathematician, social reformer

Youth is happy

because it has the ability to see beauty.

Anyone who keeps the ability to see beauty

never grows old.

Franz Kafka, 1883–1924
Czechoslovakian-born writer

I hope never to feel

completely fulfilled

because then the point of the journey

would be destroyed.

You have got to have curiosity,

hunger, and slight anxiety.

Joanna Trollope, b.1943
English novelist

*H*uman felicity is produced

not so much by

great pieces of good fortune

that seldom happen

as by little advantages

that occur every day.

Benjamin Franklin, 1706–1790
American statesman, scientist

A loving person lives in a loving world.

A hostile person lives in a hostile world.

Everyone you meet is your mirror.

Ken Keyes Jr., 1921–1995
Personal growth leader, peace advocate

*J*ust don't give up trying to do

what you really want to do.

When there is love and inspiration,

I don't think you can go far wrong.

Ella Fitzgerald, 1918–1996
American singer

In spite of illness, in spite even of the

arch-enemy sorrow, one can remain alive

long past the usual date of disintegration

if one is unafraid of change, insatiable in

intellectual curiosity, interested in big things,

and happy in small ways.

Edith Wharton, 1862–1937
American novelist

Live as if everything you do

will eventually be known.

Hugh Prather, b. 1938
American writer

*W*hat can be added

to the happiness of a man who is in health,

out of debt, and has a clear conscience?

Adam Smith, 1723–1790
Scottish economist, philosopher, essayist

$\mathcal{T}$o find out what one is fitted to do

and to secure an opportunity to do it

is the key to happiness.

John Dewey, 1859–1952
American educationalist, philosopher, reformer

I accept life unconditionally.

Most people ask for happiness on condition.

Happiness can only be felt

if you don't set any condition.

_____

Arthur Rubinstein, 1887–1982
Polish-born pianist

What Do We Live For?

*W*hat do we live for

if not to make life

less difficult for each other?

George Eliot, 1819–1880
English novelist

*W*hat is the use of living

if not to strive for noble causes

and to make this muddled world a better place

for those who will live in it after we are gone.

Sir Winston Churchill, 1874–1965
British Prime Minister, statesman

*G*etting money

is not all a man's business;

to cultivate kindness is a valuable part

of the business of life.

Samuel Johnson, 1709–1784
English lexicographer, critic, essayist

*T*he only interest in living

comes from believing in life,

from loving life, and using

all the power of your intelligence

to know it better.

Emile Zola, 1840–1902
French writer

$\mathcal{T}$he ideals that have lighted my way and,

time after time, have given me

new courage to face life cheerfully

have been Kindness, Beauty, and Truth.

Albert Einstein, 1879–1955
German-born American physicist

The perfume of sandalwood,

the scent of rosebay and jasmine,

travel only as far as the wind.

But the fragrance of goodness travels with us

through all the worlds.

Like garlands woven from a heap of flowers,

fashion your life

as a garland of beautiful deeds.

Buddha, c. 500 BC
Indian philosopher, founder of Buddhism

If I can stop

One heart from breaking,

I shall not live in vain.

If I can ease one life the aching

Or cool one pain

Or help one fainting robin

Unto his nest again,

I shall not live in vain.

Emily Dickinson, 1830–1886
American poet

*L*ife was meant to be lived.

Curiosity must be kept alive.

One must never, for whatever reason,

turn his back on life.

Eleanor Roosevelt, 1884–1962
First Lady of the United States of America

In our life, there is a single color,

as on an artist's palette, which provides

the meaning of art and life.

It is the color of love.

Marc Chagall, 1887–1985
French painter

$\mathcal{W}$ho will tell whether one happy moment
of love or the joy of breathing or walking on a bright
morning and smelling the fresh air is not worth all the
suffering and effort that life implies?

Eric Fromm, 1900–1980
American psychoanalyst

Believe that life is worth living,

and your belief will help

create the fact.

William James, 1842–1910
American psychologist, philosopher

$\mathcal{A}$t the end of your life, you will

never regret not having passed one more test,

not winning one more verdict, or

not closing one more deal.

You will regret time not spent with a husband,

a friend, a child, or parent.

Barbara Bush, b. 1925
First Lady of the United States of America

The greatest use of life

is to spend it for something

that will outlast it.

William James, 1842–1910
American psychologist, philosopher

Little deed of kindness,

Little words of love,

Help to make earth happy

Like the heaven above.

Julia Fletcher Carney, 1823–1908
American teacher

*T*he purpose of life is to matter –

to count, to stand for something,

to have it make some difference

that we lived at all.

Leo Rosten, 1908–1997
Polish-born American writer, humorist

$\mathcal{H}$e who does not live
in some degree for others
hardly lives for himself.

Michel de Montaigne, 1533–1592
French essayist

*Y*ou must understand the whole of life,

not just one little part of it.

That is why you must read;

that is why you must look at the skies;

that is why you must sing and dance

and write poems and suffer

and understand; for all that is life.

Jiddu Krishnamurti, 1895–1986
Indian theosophist

*N*o man can live happily

who regards himself alone,

who turns everything to his own advantage.

Thou must live for another

if thou wishest to live for thyself.

Seneca, c. 4 BC–65 AD
Roman philosopher, dramatist, statesman

$\mathcal{T}$he purpose of life is to live it,

to taste experience to the utmost,

to reach out eagerly and without fear

for newer and richer experience.

Eleanor Roosevelt, 1884–1962
First Lady of the United States of America

As I grow to understand life less and less,

I learn to love it more and more.

Jules Renard, 1864–1888
French writer

*T*here are two things to aim for in life:

first to get what you want

and, after that, to enjoy it.

Only the wisest of mankind

achieve the second.

Logan Pearsall Smith, 1865–1946
American-born British wit, writer, critic

$\mathscr{E}$ach player must accept the cards life deals him.

But once they are in hand,

he alone must decide how to play the cards

in order to win the game.

Voltaire, 1694–1778
French philosopher, author

Life is not made up of great sacrifices

and duties but of little things

in which smiles and kindness given habitually

are what win and preserve the heart

and secure comfort.

Sir Humphrey Davy, 1778–1829
English chemist, inventor

$\mathcal{L}$ife is a pure flame,

and we live by an invisible sun

within us.

Sir Thomas Brown, 1778–1820
Scottish metaphysician

I have never given very deep thought

to a philosophy of life, though I have

a few ideas that I think are useful to me:

Do whatever comes your way as well as you can.

Think as little as possible about yourself.

Think as much as possible about other people.

Dwell on things that are interesting.

Since you get more joy out of giving joy to others,

you should put a good deal of thought into

the happiness that you are able to give.

Eleanor Roosevelt, 1884–1962
First Lady of the United States of America

Is it so small a thing

To have enjoy'd the sun,

To have liv'd light

In the spring,

To have lov'd,

To have thought,

To have done?

Matthew Arnold, 1822–1888
English poet, essayist

$\mathcal{I}$t is one of the most beautiful
compensations of this life that no man
can sincerely try to help another
without helping himself.

Ralph Waldo Emerson, 1803–1882
American poet, essayist, teacher

$\mathscr{A}$s long as you live,

keep learning how to live.

Seneca, c. 4 BC–65AD
Roman dramatist, poet, statesman

$\mathcal{D}$oing nothing for others

is the undoing of one's self.

We must be purposely kind and generous

or we miss the best past of life's existence.

The heart that goes out of itself

gets large and full of joy.

We do ourselves most good

by doing something for others.

Horace Mann, 1796–1859
American educator, writer, politician

Words From the Wise

I expect to pass through life but once.

If, therefore, there be any kindness I can show

or any good thing I can do to any fellow being,

let me do it now,

for I shall not pass this way again.

William Penn, 1644–1718
English-born Quaker, founder of Pennsylvania

$\mathcal{W}$e act as though comfort and luxury

were the chief requirements of life

when all that we need to make us really happy

is something to be enthusiastic about.

Charles Kingsley, 1819–1875
English writer, clergyman

$\mathcal{K}$eep me away

from the wisdom which does not cry,

the philosophy which does not laugh,

and the greatness which does not bow down

before children.

Kahlil Gibran, 1883–1931
Lebanese poet, artist, mystic

*A*s you grow older,

I think you should put your arms

around each other more.

Barbara Bush, b. 1925
First Lady of the United States of America

*B*y compassion,

we make others' misery our own,

and so, by relieving them,

we relieve ourselves also.

Thomas Browne, 1605–1682
English writer, physician

$\mathscr{T}$he world is a looking-glass

and gives back to every man

the reflection of his own face.

Sir Winston Churchill, 1874–1965
British Prime Minister, statesman

$\mathcal{I}$f you achieve success,

you will get applause,

and if you get applause, you will hear it.

My advice to you concerning applause is this:

Enjoy it but never quite believe it.

Robert Montgomery, 1807–1855
English preacher, poet

$\mathcal{G}$o forth into the busy world and love it.

Interest yourself in life, mingle kindly with its joys

and sorrows, try what you can do for others rather

than what you can make them do for you,

and you will know what it is to have friends.

Ralph Waldo Emerson, 1803–1882
American poet, essayist, teacher

*I could not, at any age, be content
to take my place in a corner by the fireside
and simply look on.
Life was meant to be lived.
Curiosity must be kept alive.
The fatal thing is rejection.
One must never, for whatever reason,
turn his back on life.*

Eleanor Roosevelt, 1884–1962
First Lady of the United States of America

$\mathcal{T}$he price of anything is

the amount of life you exchange for it.

Henry David Thoreau, 1817–1862
American essayist, social critic, writer

$\mathcal{K}$eep away from people

who try to belittle your ambition.

Small people always do that,

but the really great make you feel

that you, too,

can become great.

Mark Twain, 1835–1910
American writer

To have reason to get up in the morning,

it is necessary to possess a guiding principle,

a belief of some kind,

a bumper sticker, if you will.

Judith Guest, b. 1936
American novelist

To become content,

look back on those

who possess less than yourself,

not forward to those

who possess more.

Benjamin Franklin, 1706–1790
American statesman, scientist

*S*how love to all creatures

and thou wilt be happy;

for when thou lovest all things,

thou lovest the Lord,

for He is all in all.

Hindu spiritual tradition

All that we are is the result of what we have thought:

It is founded on our thoughts; it is made up of our thoughts.

If a man speaks or acts with a pure thought, happiness

follows him like a shadow that never leaves him.

Buddha, c. 500 BC
Indian philosopher, founder of Buddhism

I do my thing

and you do your thing.

I am not in this world to live up to your expectations,

and you are not in this world to live up to mine.

You are you and I am I.

And if by chance we find each other, it's beautiful.

If not, it can't be helped.

Frederick Salomon Perls, 1893–1970
German-born American psychologist

When I look back on all these worries,
I remember the story of the old man
who said on his deathbed
that he had had a lot of trouble,
most of which never happened.

Sir Winston Churchill, 1874–1965
British Prime Minister, statesman

In matters of style,

swim with the current;

in matters of principle,

stand like a rock.

Thomas Jefferson, 1743–1826
President of the United States of America